Ruth

Discovering Your Place in God's Story

Drawn in
BIBLE STUDY

Eugene H. Peterson

THE**MESSAGE**

NavPress

A NavPress resource published in alliance with Tyndale House Publishers

NavPress is the publishing ministry of The Navigators, an international Christian organization and leader in personal spiritual development. NavPress is committed to helping people grow spiritually and enjoy lives of meaning and hope through personal and group resources that are biblically rooted, culturally relevant, and highly practical.

For more information, visit NavPress.com.

Ruth: Discovering Your Place in God's Story

Copyright © 2017 by Eugene H. Peterson. All rights reserved.

A NavPress resource published in alliance with Tyndale House Publishers

NAVPRESS, the NavPress logo, *THE MESSAGE*, and THE MESSAGE logo are registered trademarks of NavPress, The Navigators, Colorado Springs, CO. *TYNDALE* is a registered trademark of Tyndale House Ministries. Absence of ® in connection with marks of NavPress or other parties does not indicate an absence of registration of those marks.

The Team:
Don Pape, Publisher
David Zimmerman, Editor
Jennifer Ghionzoli, Designer

Cover and interior illustrations are the property of their respective copyright holders, and all rights are reserved. Cover illustration by Lizzie Preston © NavPress; cover watercolor background © Digital Goodness/Creative Market. Interior borders and other images on page 28 © Felicity French/Advocate Inc.; interior geometric pattern © Vítek Prchal/Creative Market; all other interior illustrations by Lizzie Preston, Angelika Scudamore, and Jennifer Tucker © NavPress.

The author is represented by the literary agency of Alive Literary Agency, 7680 Goddard St., Suite 200, Colorado Springs, CO 80920, www.aliveliterary.com.

All Scripture quotations are taken from *THE MESSAGE*, copyright © 1993, 1994, 1995, 1996, 2000, 2001, 2002 by Eugene H. Peterson. Used by permission of NavPress. All rights reserved. Represented by Tyndale House Publishers.

Some content from the introduction and "How to Get the Most out of Ruth" is adapted from *Eat This Book*, copyright © 2006 by Eugene H. Peterson. Published by Eerdmans. Reprinted by permission of the publisher; all rights reserved. Some content is adapted from *Five Smooth Stones for Pastoral Work*, copyright © 1992 by Eugene H. Peterson. Published by Eerdmans. Reprinted by permission of the publisher; all rights reserved. Some content from "How to Lead a Drawn In Bible Study" is adapted from Eugene H. Peterson, *The Wisdom of Each Other* (Grand Rapids, MI: Zondervan, 1998). The quotation from Tricia McCary Rhodes is from "Bible Study Meets Crafting," *Her.meneutics*, July 5, 2016, accessed July 8, 2016, at www.christianitytoday.com/women /2016/july/bible-study-meets-crafting-bible-journaling-craze.html?paging=off.

For information about special discounts for bulk purchases, please contact Tyndale House Publishers at csresponse@tyndale.com, or call 1-800-323-9400.

ISBN 978-1-63146-786-8

Printed in China

26	25	24	23	22	21	20
8	7	6	5	4	3	2

contents

introduction

Eugene H. Peterson

READING IS THE FIRST THING, just reading the Bible. As we read, we enter a new world of words and find ourselves in on a conversation in which God has the first and last words. God uses words to form and bless us, to teach and guide us, to forgive and save us.

I didn't start out as a pastor. I began my vocational life as a teacher and for several years taught the biblical languages of Hebrew and Greek in a theological seminary. I expected to live the rest of my life as a professor and scholar, teaching and writing and studying. But then my life took a sudden vocational turn to pastoring a congregation.

I was now plunged into quite a different world. The first noticeable difference was that nobody seemed to care much about the Bible, which so recently people had been paying me to teach them. Many of the people I worked with now knew virtually nothing about it, had never read it, and weren't interested in learning. Many others had spent years reading it, but for them it had gone flat through familiarity, reduced to clichés. Bored, they dropped it. And there weren't many people in between. Very few were interested in what I considered my primary work, getting the words of the Bible into their heads and hearts, getting the message lived. They found newspapers and magazines, videos and pulp fiction more to their taste.

Meanwhile I had taken on as my life work the responsibility for getting these very people to listen—really listen—to the message in this book. I knew I had my work cut out for me.

I lived in two language worlds, the world of the Bible and the world of today. I had always assumed they were the same world. But these people didn't see it that way. So out of necessity I became a "translator" (although I wouldn't have called it that then), daily standing on the border between two worlds, getting the language of the Bible that God uses to create and save us, heal and bless us, judge and rule over us, into the language of today that we use to gossip and tell stories, give directions and do business, sing songs and talk to our children.

My intent is simply to get people reading the Bible who don't know that the Bible is readable at all, at least by them, and to get people who long ago lost interest in the Bible to read it again. Read in order to live, praying as you read, "God, let it be with me just as you say."

INTRODUCTION TO RUTH

As we read the broad, comprehensive biblical story of God at work in the world, most of us are entirely impressed: God speaking creation into being, God laying the foundations of the life of faith through great and definitive fathers and mothers, God saving a people out of a brutal slave existence and then forming them into lives of free and obedient love, God raising up leaders who direct and guide through the tangle of difficulties always involved in living joyfully and responsively before God.

Very impressive. So impressive, in fact, that many of us, while remaining impressed, feel left out. Our unimpressive, very ordinary lives make us feel like outsiders to such a star-studded cast. We disqualify ourselves. Guilt or willfulness or accident makes a loophole, and we assume that what is true for everyone else is not true for us. We conclude that we are, somehow, "just not religious" and thus unfit to participate in the big story.

And then we turn a page and come on this small story of two widows and a farmer in their out-of-the-way village.

The unknown author, a master of the short story, wrote sometime after the reign of David, Ruth's great-grandson.

Ancient literature focused on men, especially powerful men, so it's extraordinary to get a tale from the point of view of two lower-class women. The outsider Ruth was not born into the faith and felt no natural part of it—like many of us. But she came to find herself gathered into the story and given a quiet and obscure part that proved critical to the way everything turned out.

Scripture is a vast tapestry of God's creating, saving, and blessing ways in this world. The great names in the plot that climaxes at Sinai (Abraham, Isaac, Jacob, Joseph, Moses) and the great names in the sequel (Joshua, Samuel, David, Solomon) can be intimidating to ordinary, random individuals: "Surely there is no way that I can have any significant part on such a stage." But the story of the widowed, impoverished alien Ruth is proof to the contrary. She is the inconsequential outsider whose life turns out to be essential for telling the complete story of God's ways among us. The unassuming ending carries the punch line: Boaz married Ruth, she had a son, Obed; Obed was the father of Jesse, and Jesse the father of David.

David! In its artful telling of this "outsider" widow, uprooted and obscure, who turns out to be the great-grandmother of David and the ancestor of Jesus, the book of Ruth makes it possible for each of us to understand ourselves, however ordinary or "out of it," as irreplaceable in the full telling of God's story. We count—every last one of us—and what we do counts.

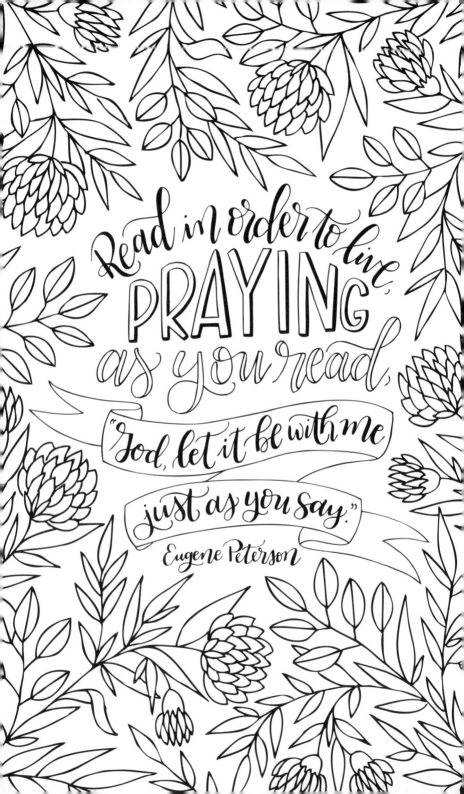

Read in order to live,
PRAYING
as you read,
"God, let it be with me
just as you say."

Eugene Peterson

HOW TO GET THE MOST OUT OF

*It takes more than bread
to stay alive. It takes a steady stream
of words from God's mouth.*

MATTHEW 4:4

MANY PEOPLE APPROACH READING the Bible as a religious duty or a way to get in good with God. Worse still, some believe God will send a horrible punishment if they don't dedicate at least a half hour each day to dutiful study of his Word. Coming to the Bible with so much religious baggage takes all the fun out of reading it.

Reading the Bible isn't simply a fact-finding mission. You don't come just to collect bits of trivia about God. From the moment you read the first line of the Bible, you will discover that this book isn't about you. It's about God. God gave his Word as the place where you meet him face-to-face.

In order to read the Scriptures adequately and

accurately, it's necessary at the same time to live them—to live them *as* we read them. This kind of reading has been named by our ancestors as *lectio divina*, often translated "spiritual reading." It means not only reading the text but also meditating on the text, praying the text, and living the text. It is reading that enters our souls the way food enters our stomachs, spreads through our blood, and transforms us. Christians don't simply learn or study or use Scripture; we feed on it. Words spoken and listened to, written and read are intended to do something in us, to give us health and wholeness, vitality and holiness, wisdom and hope.

The Scriptures not only reveal everything of who God is but also everything of who we are. And this revelation is done in such a way as to invite participation on both sides, of author and reader.

This may be the single most important thing to know as we come to read and study and believe these Holy Scriptures: this rich, alive, personally revealing God as experienced in Father, Son, and Holy Spirit, personally addressing us in whatever circumstances we find ourselves, at whatever age we are, in whatever state we are. Christian reading is participatory reading, receiving the words in such a way that they become interior to our lives, the rhythms and images becoming practices of prayer, acts of obedience, ways of love. We submit our lives to this text so that God's will may be done on earth as it is in heaven.

One of the characteristic marks of the biblical story-tellers is a certain reticence. They don't tell us too much. They leave a lot of blanks in the narration, an implicit invitation to enter the story ourselves, just as we are, and to discover for ourselves how to fit in. There are, of course, always moral, theological, and historical elements in these stories that need to be studied, but never in dismissal of the story that is being told.

When we submit our lives to what we read in Scripture, we find that we're being led not to see God in our stories but to see our stories in God's. God is the larger context and plot in which our stories find themselves.

The Bible is God's Word. He spoke it into existence and he continues to speak through it as you read. He doesn't just share words on a page. He shares himself. As you meet God in this conversation, you won't just learn *about* him; you will *experience* him more deeply and more personally than you ever thought possible.

DRAWN IN BIBLE STUDIES

We all lead busy lives, and even when we step away from our activities for spiritual rest and renewal, our activities don't necessarily step away from us. *Drawn in* Bible Studies are designed to temporarily relieve you of distractions so you can enjoy the story of God more fully. This happens in a variety of ways:

The Coloring

For people of all ages, coloring offers a structured activity that fosters creative thinking. Tricia McCary Rhodes, author of *The Wired Soul*, is not surprised by the appeal of coloring among adults today:

> Brain scans of people involved in activities like coloring reveal that as we focus, our heart rate slows and our brain waves enter a more relaxed state. Over time, by engaging in Scripture or prayer art-journaling, it may become easier for us to focus and pay attention in other areas of our lives as well. It is no wonder we are so drawn to this activity.

As you work through a study, read the appropriate Bible passage and question, and mull over your response as you color. Some art has been provided for you, but feel free to draw in the open space as well. The act of coloring will help your "orienting response," the brain function that allows you to filter out background distractions and attend to the matter at hand. That's one reason so many people doodle as they read or study. Ironically, by coloring as you engage in this Bible study, you'll be more attentive to what the Scriptures have to teach you.

The Message

For many people, the Bible has become so familiar that it loses some of its resonance. They've memorized so many Scriptures, or heard so many sermons, that they think they've figured a passage out. For others, the Bible has never not been intimidating—its names and contexts separated from us by millennia, its story shrouded by memories of bad church experiences or negative impressions of people who claim it as their authority. While you can read any Bible translation you like alongside the *Drawn in* Bible Studies, included in the studies themselves are passages from *The Message*, a rendering of the Bible in contemporary language that matches the tone and informality of the original, ancient language. You will often be surprised by the way *The Message* translates something you may have read or heard many times before. And in that surprise, you'll be more receptive for what God might have for you today.

The Questions

When we sit down just to read the Bible, we can feel a bit disoriented. The questions in the *Drawn in* Bible Studies are designed to help you stay connected to your own lived experience even as you enter into the lived experience of the people and places the Scriptures introduce us to. You'll grow in your understanding of the Bible, but you'll also grow in your understanding of yourself. These questions are also good for discussion—get together with a group of friends, and enjoy coloring and talking together.

The Commentary

Included in this *Drawn in* Bible Study are occasional comments from renowned Bible teacher Eugene Peterson. You'll see his name following his comments. He helps clarify more confusing passages and offers insight into what's behind what you're reading. He'll help keep you from getting stuck.

Leader's Notes

In the section "How to Lead a *Drawn in* Bible Study" you'll find general guidelines for leading people through this study, along with notes specific to each session. These can inform and enhance your experience, so even if you are going through this study on your own, or if you are not the leader of a group discussion of this study, read through the notes as preparation for each session. Nevertheless, don't feel pressure to be an expert; the main purpose of this study is to provide an opportunity for fun and fellowship as people encounter God's Word and consider how it touches their lives.

God Has Dealt Me a Hard Blow

RUTH 1

THE BOOK OF Ruth is only a sample of what's possible when we take the stories of other people seriously. It offers evidence that it can be done and provides the stimulus for others to do it. Every one of us, though, has to find his or her own way into the story.

—EUGENE

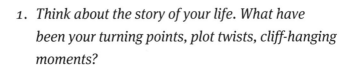

1. *Think about the story of your life. What have been your turning points, plot twists, cliff-hanging moments?*

2. *How have you changed over the course of the story?*

3. *Reflect on specific people you have met along the way. How have those people affected your story?*

   How have you affected theirs?

ONCE UPON A time—it was back in the days when judges led Israel—there was a famine in the land. A man from Bethlehem in Judah left home to live in the country of Moab, he and his wife and his two sons. The man's name was Elimelech; his wife's name was Naomi; his sons were named Mahlon and Kilion—all Ephrathites from Bethlehem in Judah. They all went to the country of Moab and settled there.

Elimelech died and Naomi was left, she and her two sons. The sons took Moabite wives; the name of the first was Orpah, the second Ruth. They lived there in Moab for the next ten years. But then the two brothers, Mahlon and Kilion, died. Now the woman was left without either her young men or her husband.

One day she got herself together, she and her two daughters-in-law, to leave the country of Moab and set out for home; she had heard that GOD had been pleased to visit his people and give them food. And so she started out from the place she had been living, she and her two daughters-in-law with her, on the road back to the land of Judah.

RUTH 1:1-7

4. *Elimelech took his family out of Judah because of a famine. Recall a time you were tempted to leave a hard situation. Did you leave or stay? Why?*

Do you think Elimelech made the right decision to leave Bethlehem? Why or why not?

5. *Life didn't get easier for Elimelech or his family. A lot of pain is condensed into three verses (verses 3-5). Sometimes it seems like a lot of pain has been condensed into our lives as well. What have you been taught or told about how to deal with pain and loss?*

How do you relate to God when you're dealing with pain or loss?

6. *Why does Naomi decide to return to Judah? How does this compare to her family's decision to leave Judah in the first place?*

7. *Think of a "Naomi moment" you've had—a moment when you were forced by circumstance to make a hard choice. What choices did you have to make? What did you feel as you went through the process?*

What helped to guide your decision?

—————— ✂ ——————

*A*FTER A SHORT while on the road, Naomi told her two daughters-in-law, "Go back. Go home and live with your mothers. And may GOD treat you as graciously as you treated your deceased husbands and me. May GOD give each of you a new home and a new husband!" She kissed them and they cried openly.

They said, "No, we're going on with you to your people."

But Naomi was firm: "Go back, my dear daughters. Why would you come with me? Do you suppose I still have sons in my womb who can become your future husbands? Go back, dear daughters—on your way, please! I'm too old to get a husband. Why, even if I said, 'There's still hope!' and this very night got a man and had sons, can you imagine being satisfied to wait until they were grown? Would you wait that long to get married again? No, dear daughters; this is a bitter pill for me to swallow—more bitter for me than for you. God has dealt me a hard blow."

Again they cried openly. Orpah kissed her mother-in-law good-bye; but Ruth embraced her and held on.

Naomi said, "Look, your sister-in-law is going back home to live with her own people and gods; go with her."

But Ruth said, "Don't force me to leave you; don't make me go home. Where you go, I go; and where you live, I'll live. Your people are my people, your God is my god; where you die, I'll die, and that's where I'll be buried, so help me GOD—not even death itself is going to come between us!"

"GOD HAS DEALT ME A HARD BLOW."

FROM RUTH 1, MSG

When Naomi saw that Ruth had her heart set on going with her, she gave in. And so the two of them traveled on together to Bethlehem.

RUTH 1:8-19 ————————————————

8. *At first Naomi brings her daughters-in-law along with her, but then she tells them to "go back." Explain her rationale for parting with Ruth and Orpah. What would you have done?*

9. *In what ways do you identify with Ruth?*

10. *Who in your life would you stick with, no matter what? Why?*

11. *In what ways do you identify with Orpah?*

12. *Reflect on a relationship or friendship in your life that ended. What was hard about that ending? How has your life changed since?*

WHEN THEY ARRIVED in Bethlehem the whole town was soon buzzing: "Is this really our Naomi? And after all this time!"

But she said, "Don't call me Naomi; call me Bitter. The Strong One has dealt me a bitter blow. I left here full of life, and GOD has brought me back with nothing but the clothes on my back. Why would you call me Naomi? God certainly doesn't. The Strong One ruined me."

And so Naomi was back, and Ruth the foreigner with her, back from the country of Moab. They arrived in Bethlehem at the beginning of the barley harvest.

RUTH 1:19-22 ————————————————

13. *Naomi had to leave her family and her home, and then in a strange land she lost her husband and her sons. One hard thing after another. In what ways do you identify with Naomi?*

"Your people are my people, your God is my god."

From Ruth 1, MSG

🖎 **NAOMI GOT INTO** the story by complaining. She
A NOTE
FROM
EUGENE
experienced loss, complained bitterly about it, and
had her unhappiness taken seriously by a storyteller
who formed it into a complaint against God.

---

14. *Does it surprise you to read Naomi's complaint*
    "The Strong One ruined me"? Why?

When we see that God's Word includes complaints
against him, what do we learn about him?

15. *Are you tempted to defend God against Naomi?*
    Why or why not?

A NOTE
FROM
EUGENE

FORMALIZED COMPLAINTS ARE common in Scripture. As people looking to help others find their way in their story, we don't always have to be on God's side, defending him. There are in fact times when the biblical position is at the plaintiff's side.

16. *Reflect on a time you or a loved one complained about God. What feelings were underneath the complaint? Did your understanding of God change in that situation? How?*

How do you think God responds to our complaints?

Until we meet again

CONTINUE TO REFLECT *on your life story. In what situations do you now see God's role differently than you did at first? Take some time to acknowledge God's part in your story, and ask God to help you play a strong supporting role in the stories of your loved ones.*

KEEP AN EYE *out for people who need help telling their stories. Consider when you are called to play the role of God's defender, or when you might be called to help give voice to a complaint against God.*

Consider scheduling a time to "swap stories" with someone. Give the other person a chance to share his or her Naomi moments, including difficult feelings about God, and be prepared to share your own.

Prayer

Thank you, Lord, for the providential way you have guided my life,

> *though at times it's been hard to see the providence*
>> *for all the plot twists.*

Help me to be brave and good and true,

> *regardless of where the story takes me.*

Help me to be a good listener to other people's stories,

> *being attentive to what you're doing*
>> *in them and around them.*

Don't Worry about a Thing

RUTH 2

BY TAKING EVERYDAY things in a serious vein,
we discover an inner structure revealed in them.
People and events that appear on the surface to
enter the story randomly are actually embedded in
the strata of salvation history. We just have to dig a
little below the surface to find them.

—EUGENE

1. *Recall a time things seemed to work out surprisingly well for you. How did you explain your success at the time?*

2. *As you look back now, what role did that experience play in your larger story? What did it tell you about yourself, your circumstances, or God?*

———————— ❧ ————————

IT SO HAPPENED that Naomi had a relative by marriage, a man prominent and rich, connected with Elimelech's family. His name was Boaz.

One day Ruth, the Moabite foreigner, said to Naomi, "I'm going to work; I'm going out to glean among the sheaves, following after some harvester who will treat me kindly."

Naomi said, "Go ahead, dear daughter."

And so she set out. She went and started gleaning in a field, following in the wake of the harvesters. Eventually she ended up in the part of the field owned by Boaz, her father-in-law Elimelech's relative. A little later Boaz came out from Bethlehem, greeting his harvesters, "GOD be with you!" They replied, "And GOD bless you!"

Boaz asked his young servant who was foreman over the farm hands, "Who is this young woman? Where did she come from?"

The foreman said, "Why, that's the Moabite girl, the one who came with Naomi from the country of Moab. She asked permission. 'Let me glean,' she said, 'and gather among the sheaves following after your harvesters.' She's been at it steady ever since, from early morning until now, without so much as a break."

RUTH 2:1-7 ————————————————————

3. *Now in Judah, the story shifts its focus from Naomi, who is back in her homeland, to Ruth, who is a stranger here. What do you learn about Ruth in the opening passage of Ruth 2 (verses 2-4)?*

4. *Ruth and Naomi's poverty is contrasted here with the wealth and prominence of Boaz. What are your first impressions of him (see verses 1-5)?*

5. *What impresses the foreman about Ruth?*

6. *We saw in chapter 1 that "the whole town was soon buzzing" (verses 18-19) about Naomi and Ruth. And yet gleaning leftover crops is humbling work. How would you have felt in Ruth's place, doing such lowly work in such a conspicuous way?*

Think of some people you know who are doing humbling work. What makes their work humbling? What do you admire about them?

———————— ✄ ————————

THEN BOAZ SPOKE to Ruth: "Listen, my daughter. From now on don't go to any other field to glean—stay right here in this one. And stay close to my young women. Watch where they are harvesting and follow them. And don't worry about a thing; I've given orders to my servants not to harass you. When you get thirsty, feel free to go and drink from the water buckets that the servants have filled."

She dropped to her knees, then bowed her face to the ground. "How does this happen that you should pick me out and treat me so kindly—*me*, a foreigner?"

Boaz answered her, "I've heard all about you—heard about the way you treated your mother-in-law after the death of her husband, and how you left your father and mother and the land of your birth and have come to live among a bunch of total strangers. God reward you well for what you've done—and with a generous bonus besides from God, to whom you've come seeking protection under his wings."

She said, "Oh sir, such grace, such kindness—I don't deserve it. You've touched my heart, treated me like one of your own. And I don't even belong here!"

At the lunch break, Boaz said to her, "Come over here; eat some bread. Dip it in the wine."

So she joined the harvesters. Boaz passed the roasted grain to her. She ate her fill and even had some left over.

When she got up to go back to work, Boaz ordered his servants: "Let her glean where there's still plenty of grain on the ground—make it easy for her. Better yet, pull some of the good stuff out and leave it for her to glean. Give her special treatment."

RUTH 2:8-16————————————

7. What impresses Boaz about Ruth (see verses 11-12)? How is this different from the impression she's made on others?

What impresses you about Ruth?

8. What impresses Ruth about Boaz (see verses 10, 13)?

What impresses you about Boaz?

9. Think of someone you know who has power and authority. What do you admire about them? Is it their position or their character? Why?

THERE'S A REMARKABLE correspondence in Ruth, where the storyteller worked out a connection between the way God acts and the way the people in the story act. In chapter 2, Boaz introduced Ruth to God, describing him as the one "to whom you've come seeking protection under his wings" (verse 12). Later, Ruth asked Boaz, "Take me under your protecting wing" (3:9), a reference to being covered by his garment. The word "wing" in these two passages is the same word in Hebrew, forcing a recognition between what Boaz promised that God would do for Ruth and what Ruth got Boaz to do for her.

10. *Boaz didn't merely accommodate Ruth's basic needs. He went far beyond normal practice to provide for her. Note the various ways Boaz made Ruth's life easier in chapter 2.*

How can you use your position in society to bless others as Boaz did?

11. Ruth experienced Boaz's kindness, but she kept working all day long. What does this say about Ruth's character?

12. What are the virtues coded into the book of Ruth so far?

Who do you know who exhibits these virtues? Where might they be applied in your life?

*R*UTH GLEANED IN the field until evening. When she threshed out what she had gathered, she ended up with nearly a full sack of barley! She gathered up her gleanings, went back to town, and showed her mother-in-law the results of her day's work; she also gave her the leftovers from her lunch.

Naomi asked her, "So where did you glean today? Whose field? GOD bless whoever it was who took such good care of you!"

Ruth told her mother-in-law, "The man with whom I worked today? His name is Boaz."

Naomi said to her daughter-in-law, "Why, GOD bless that man! GOD hasn't quite walked out on us after all! He still loves us, in bad times as well as good!"

Naomi went on, "That man, Ruth, is one of our circle of covenant redeemers, a close relative of ours!"

Ruth the Moabitess said, "Well, listen to this: He also told me, 'Stick with my workers until my harvesting is finished.'"

Naomi said to Ruth, "That's wonderful, dear daughter! Do that! You'll be safe in the company of his young women; no danger now of being raped in some stranger's field."

So Ruth did it—she stuck close to Boaz's young women, gleaning in the fields daily until both the barley and wheat harvesting were finished. And she continued living with her mother-in-law.

RUTH 2:17-23

"God hasn't quite walked out on us after all!"

from Ruth 2, THE MESSAGE

13. *We return to Naomi at the end of chapter 2. How do you see Naomi changing over the course of these first two chapters in the book of Ruth?*

14. *Naomi offers a declaration of faith: "GOD hasn't quite walked out on us after all! He still loves us, in bad times as well as good!" What has happened to cause Naomi to change her opinion of God?*

15. *Naomi declares that God loves us "in bad times as well as good!" And yet she and Ruth are not quite out of the woods yet. What is it about good news that makes it easier to believe good things about God?*

16. *Chapter 2 ends with Ruth a permanent fixture in Boaz's fields, gleaning the leftovers from his harvest. Would this be a happy ending for you? Why or why not?*

What more do you want for Ruth?

17. *Reflect on a time when God's grace for you was delivered or demonstrated to you by someone close to you. How do you see God working in and through the lives of your loved ones?*

A NOTE FROM EUGENE

AND SO, IN this most human of encounters, divine providence was at work. God was behind the scenes, working out his will, mysteriously but magnificently, through the will of others.

Until we meet again

KEEP AN EYE OUT *for someone who's working hard at thankless work. Then thank them for it, or praise them to their supervisor.*

REFLECT *on how God has shown love to you in both good and bad times. Thank God for those demonstrations of love.*

EXPRESS *appreciation to someone who has shown kindness to you or someone you care about.*

Prayer

God, thank you for seeing and serving people like Ruth, people whose needs are so significant and whose resources are so few.

Thank you for dignifying people like Ruth, whose character was not dependent on her circumstances.

Thank you for seeding our world with your character, that we may experience Boaz-impulses toward generosity and kindness and act on them.

Give us heightened awareness of your activity in our lives.

But more than that, give us heightened awareness of the people around us—their needs, their sorrows—and the ways in which you have prepared us to be used by you to serve them.

Maybe It's Time to Make Our Move

RUTH 3

RUTH GOT INTO the story by asking for what she wanted. When the time came, Ruth took the initiative.

—EUGENE

1. *When do you find it hard to take the initiative?*

What keeps you from asking for what you want?

———————— ✶ ————————

ONE DAY HER mother-in-law Naomi said to Ruth, "My dear daughter, isn't it about time I arranged a good home for you so you can have a happy life? And isn't Boaz our close relative, the one with whose young women you've been working? Maybe it's time to make our move. Tonight is the night of Boaz's barley harvest at the threshing floor.

"Take a bath. Put on some perfume. Get all dressed up and go to the threshing floor. But don't let him know you're there until the party is well under way and he's had plenty of food and drink. When you see him slipping off to sleep, watch where he lies down and then go there. Lie at his feet to let him know that you are available to him for marriage. Then wait and see what he says. He'll tell you what to do."

Ruth said, "If you say so, I'll do it, just as you've told me."

She went down to the threshing floor and put her mother-in-law's plan into action.

RUTH 3:1-6 ————————————————

"MAYBE it's time to MAKE OUR move."

from Ruth 3,
THE MESSAGE

2. *Naomi seems different, doesn't she? How would you describe her attitude at the beginning of this chapter?*

How does it compare to her attitude in previous chapters?

3. *Ruth and her mother-in-law knew that if they played their cards right, Ruth could get a husband and they could both be rescued from poverty. Reflect on a time when you saw an opportunity—a new job, for example, or a new relationship—and had to prepare for it. What gave you hope?*

4. *How would you describe Naomi's plan? What about it makes sense to you?*

What about it makes you uncomfortable?

———————— ✄ ————————

BOAZ HAD A good time, eating and drinking his fill— he felt great. Then he went off to get some sleep, lying down at the end of a stack of barley. Ruth quietly followed; she lay down to signal her availability for marriage.

In the middle of the night the man was suddenly startled and sat up. Surprise! This woman asleep at his feet!

He said, "And who are you?"

She said, "I am Ruth, your maiden; take me under your protecting wing. You're my close relative, you know, in the circle of covenant redeemers—you do have the right to marry me."

He said, "GOD bless you, my dear daughter! What a splendid expression of love! And when you could have had your pick of any of the young men around. And now, my dear daughter, don't you worry about a thing; I'll do all you could want or ask. Everybody in town knows what a courageous woman you are—a real prize! You're right, I am a close relative to you, but there is one even closer than I am. So stay the rest of the night. In the morning, if he wants to exercise his customary rights and responsibilities as the closest covenant redeemer, he'll have his chance; but if he isn't interested, as GOD lives, I'll do it. Now go back to sleep until morning."

Ruth slept at his feet until dawn, but she got up while it was still dark and wouldn't be recognized. Then Boaz said to himself, "No one must know that Ruth came to the threshing floor."

So Boaz said, "Bring the shawl you're wearing and spread it out."

She spread it out and he poured it full of barley, six measures, and put it on her shoulders. Then she went back to town.

RUTH 3:7-15 —————————————————

5. *When have you relied on the actions and interventions of others to make something happen for you? When have you taken matters into your own hands?*

How do you decide between the two?

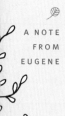

A NOTE
FROM
EUGENE

RUTH DID EXACTLY what her mother-in-law told her to do. Except for the last item. Naomi told Ruth to lie submissively at Boaz's feet. But when the time came, Ruth took the initiative and told Boaz what *she* wanted *him* to do. Being in God's story doesn't mean passively letting things happen to us. It doesn't mean dumb submission or blind obedience.

"Don't you worry about a thing."

from Ruth 3,
THE MESSAGE

6. Ruth's making herself available to Boaz was a risk; her direct appeal was even riskier. Ruth was saying, "I want you to marry me." What have we learned about Boaz to this point that makes this a risk worth taking?

How do you identify risks worth taking in your own life?

7. Boaz tells Ruth, "Everybody in town knows what a courageous woman you are—a real prize!" (verses 10-13). It's been said that the harder you work, the luckier you get. What have we learned about Ruth to this point that makes Boaz's response to her so appropriate?

8. This is the second time Boaz tells Ruth, "Don't worry about a thing" (the first time was in chapter 2). Why might Boaz repeat this? Why might Ruth need to hear it?

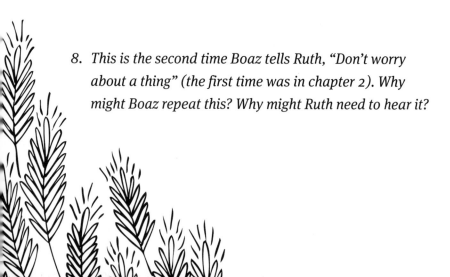

9. *How often do you struggle with worry? What helps you to reach the point where you "don't worry about a thing"?*

WHEN SHE CAME to her mother-in-law, Naomi asked, "And how did things go, my dear daughter?"

Ruth told her everything that the man had done for her, adding, "And he gave me all this barley besides—six quarts! He told me, 'You can't go back empty-handed to your mother-in-law!'"

Naomi said, "Sit back and relax, my dear daughter, until we find out how things turn out; that man isn't going to fool around. Mark my words, he's going to get everything wrapped up today."

RUTH 3:16-18

10. *Naomi had the first word in this chapter—"Maybe it's time to make our move." She also has the last word: "Sit back and relax." What do you find challenging about "making a move"?*

11. *What do you find challenging about sitting back and relaxing?*

12. *Where is God in chapter 3? In what ways is this a God-story?*

Until we meet again

PAY ATTENTION *to the people around you.*
Who could you encourage in their struggle with worry?

PAY ATTENTION *to your own circumstances—the*
opportunities and challenges you're facing this week. Ask
God to help you discern when to take initiative, when to rely
on the support of others, and when to wait for him to act.

DO SOMETHING *to show gratitude to some of the*
people in your life who have helped you succeed.

Prayer

*God, we are thankful for the ways you provide for us—
ways we aren't even aware of.*

*You're the scripter of our stories, and the little
coincidences that turn the tide in our favor are in a real
way evidence that you're writing a good story for us.*

Thank you that we can see ourselves in Ruth.

*Help us also to see ourselves in Boaz, and, like Boaz,
to look for opportunities to see others in their need, to care
for them as we are able, and to recognize the common
thread between us: that we and they are your creation,
made in your image.*

He'll Make You Young Again!

RUTH 4

THE STORY OF Ruth and Boaz wasn't simply a small love story into which they had accidentally fallen; rather it was a sprawling love story of epic proportions. For through the union of Ruth and Boaz came David. And through David came the Savior of the world.

—EUGENE

1. *Think back on your life. What was one event that seemed insignificant at the time, but that over time has proved to be significant for you and for others?*

———————— ✂ ————————

*B*OAZ WENT STRAIGHT to the public square and took his place there. Before long the "closer relative," the one mentioned earlier by Boaz, strolled by.

"Step aside, old friend," said Boaz. "Take a seat." The man sat down.

Boaz then gathered ten of the town elders together and said, "Sit down here with us; we've got some business to take care of." And they sat down.

Boaz then said to his relative, "The piece of property that belonged to our relative Elimelech is being sold by his widow Naomi, who has just returned from the country of Moab. I thought you ought to know about it. Buy it back if you want it—you can make it official in the presence of those sitting here and before the town elders. You have first redeemer rights. If you don't want it, tell me so I'll know where I stand. You're first in line to do this and I'm next after you."

He said, "I'll buy it."

Then Boaz added, "You realize, don't you, that when you buy the field from Naomi, you also get Ruth the Moabite, the widow of our dead relative, along with the redeemer responsibility to have children with her to carry on the family inheritance."

Then the relative said, "Oh, I can't do that—I'd jeopardize my own family's inheritance. You go ahead and buy it—you can have my rights—I can't do it."

In the olden times in Israel, this is how they handled official business regarding matters of property and inheritance: A man would take off his shoe and give it to the other person. This was the same as an official seal or personal signature in Israel.

So when Boaz's "redeemer" relative said, "Go ahead and buy it," he signed the deal by pulling off his shoe.

Boaz then addressed the elders and all the people in the town square that day: "You are witnesses today that I have bought from Naomi everything that belonged to Elimelech and Kilion and Mahlon, including responsibility for Ruth the foreigner, the widow of Mahlon—I'll take her as my wife and keep the name of the deceased alive along with his inheritance. The memory and reputation of the deceased is not going to disappear out of this family or from his hometown. To all this you are witnesses this very day."

All the people in the town square that day, backing up the elders, said, "Yes, we are witnesses. May GOD make this woman who is coming into your household like Rachel and Leah, the two women who built the family of Israel.

May GOD make you a pillar in Ephrathah and famous in Bethlehem! With the children GOD gives you from this young woman, may your family rival the family of Perez, the son Tamar bore to Judah."

RUTH 4:1-12 ————————————————

2. *Reflect on our culture today. Who are some powerful people who remind you of Boaz? What about them reminds you of him?*

3. *Boaz gets right to business here, but he remains cheerful and relational. Before anything else, Boaz was represented in the story as a person on good terms with the people around him. How might his example inform the way we relate to people on a day-to-day basis?*

4. *The logistics of the "covenant redeemer" arrangement come into closer focus here. Why does Boaz have to go to this man before doing what he wants?*

5. *Boaz runs the risk of losing Ruth here. What prevents the man from taking Boaz's place as her covenant redeemer?*

6. *Why does this discussion have to take place in front of the town elders?*

7. *After the man formally declines his covenant redeemer responsibilities, Boaz announces that he has "bought from Naomi everything . . . including responsibility for Ruth" (verses 9-10). We've actually not seen any interaction between Boaz and Naomi. What differences strike you between this ancient culture and our own?*

A NOTE FROM EUGENE

BOAZ COULD HAVE made the decision to dodge his responsibilities. But instead, he lived up to his name: "In him is strength." The story gave Boaz the opportunity to live up to his responsibilities. And like a hero, he seized it.

"Blessed be God! He didn't leave you without FAMILY."

FROM RUTH 4,
THE MESSAGE

———————— ✀ ————————

OAZ MARRIED RUTH. She became his wife. Boaz slept with her. By GOD's gracious gift she conceived and had a son.

The town women said to Naomi, "Blessed be GOD! He didn't leave you without family to carry on your life. May this baby grow up to be famous in Israel! He'll make you young again! He'll take care of you in old age. And this daughter-in-law who has brought him into the world and loves you so much, why, she's worth more to you than seven sons!"

Naomi took the baby and held him in her arms, cuddling him, cooing over him, waiting on him hand and foot.

The neighborhood women started calling him "Naomi's baby boy!" But his real name was Obed. Obed was the father of Jesse, and Jesse the father of David.

This is the family tree of Perez:

> Perez had Hezron,
> Hezron had Ram,
> Ram had Amminadab,
> Amminadab had Nahshon,
> Nahshon had Salmon,
> Salmon had Boaz,
> Boaz had Obed,
> Obed had Jesse,
> and Jesse had David.

RUTH 4:13-22————————

BOAZ had OBED, OBED had JESSE, —AND— JESSE had DAVID.

FROM Ruth 4, MSG

8. In what ways is Boaz a hero in this story?

How about Naomi?

How about Ruth?

9. In what ways is God a hero in this story?

10. Naomi is celebrated by the townspeople at the end of this book. The broader community plays a significant role in the story. How would you describe the role of the community? Why do you think the community's role is so big?

A NOTE
FROM
EUGENE
RUTH AND BOAZ had a son, whom the townspeople called "Naomi's baby boy" (verse 17). That boy became the grandfather of David, Israel's second king and a direct ancestor of Jesus. The storyteller, who attached the genealogical conclusion, was thoroughly aware of the impact it would have on Jewish readers.

11. *How does your own story connect to your larger community? In what ways do you wish it would?*

12. *Is the book of Ruth a small story or a big story? Or both? Why?*

13. *How conscious do you think Ruth was of the larger story she was a part of? How would the rituals and community that make up a big part of this story help her to think of that larger context?*

14. *What helps you to think about your story in the larger context of God's work in the world?*

   What habits would help you to keep that in mind more consistently?

15. *What do you want to remember from the book of Ruth—about character? About God's provision? About how individual people fit into God's story?*

Until we meet again

TAKE SOME TIME *to reflect on and journal through some of the hard stories of your past. What got you through them? What can you point to in those stories that suggests God was at work in your life?*

JOURNAL *through some of the hard things you're facing now. What evidence can you see to suggest that God is at work? What larger work might you be a part of?*

WHO ARE *the people around you who have come through hard times? Think of some ways you can celebrate them the way the neighborhood women celebrated Naomi.*

Prayer

Thank you, Lord, for the providential way you have guided my life,

> *though at times it's been hard to see the providence*
> > *for all the plot twists.*

Help me to be brave and good and true,

> *regardless of where the story takes me.*

Help me to be a good listener to other people's stories,

> *being attentive to what you're doing*
> > *in them and around them.*

The Scriptures not only reveal EVERYTHING of who God is — BUT ALSO — EVERYTHING of who we are.

Eugene Peterson

Drawn in

BIBLE STUDY

THE DOMINANT AND OBVIOUS forms of Christian discourse are preaching and teaching. That is as it should be. We have a great event of salvation to announce to the world. And we have a revealed truth about God and ourselves that we need to make as plain as possible. But there are other ways of using words that are just as important, if not as conspicuous: questions and conversations, comments and ruminations, counsel and suggestion. It's a quieter use of language and mostly takes place in times and locations that aren't set apart for religious discourse. It's the quieter conversational give-and-take of relationships in which we take each other seriously, respectfully attentive to what is said to us and thoughtfully responsive in what we say in return.

Our conversations with each other are sacred. Those that take place in the parking lot after Sunday worship are as much a part of the formation of Christian character as the preaching. But conversation, as such, is much neglected today as a form of Christian discourse. If we're to be in touch with all the parts of our lives and all the dimensions of the gospel, conversation requires equal billing (although not equal authority) with preaching and teaching.

The *Drawn in* Bible Studies can be a wonderful resource for personal Bible study. But because conversation is so valuable to our spiritual growth, consider working through the *Drawn in* Bible Studies with a group. Doing these studies together can be a wonderful way of enriching each person's understanding of the Scriptures, as well as an opportunity to grow deeper in relationship. Any number of benefits come from studying the Bible together, for example:

- New insights into God's Word
- Mutual encouragement
- Prayer for one another
- More robust relationships

These Bible studies are particularly good "on-ramps" for people who are new to the Bible, the practice of group or individual Bible study, or even the Christian faith. Non-Christians and new believers can be great participants in these studies, both for their own spiritual growth and for their fresh perspectives on what can be, for seasoned Bible study participants, overly familiar territory.

These Bible studies will also be rewarding for people of all levels of spiritual maturity, offering a more reflective, creative approach to the small-group context.

As a leader, you will set the tone and manage the expectations of all participants. Not only the material you discuss but the environment you create for your group will send a message about who God is and how he relates to people. So give thought to how your meeting space can be warm and welcoming, how it can communicate compassion and care.

Because some questions invite vulnerability, and because people can be insecure about expressing their creative side, you'll want to establish and regularly reinforce the idea of grace and compassion as foundational to your group. Consider developing a "Bible study covenant" that each participant commits to, emphasizing these virtues. You'll also want to model vulnerability in how you engage the questions as they come up.

Your main job is to facilitate conversation. The study guide is a resource to that end. The questions are designed to be read out loud. Feel free to skip or rephrase a question if it seems out of sync with the overall discussion. If your group discussion is particularly robust, feel the freedom to select only a few key questions from each chapter. Be sure to allow time and space for group members to raise their own questions about the passage you're studying.

You'll also want to manage people's expectations. Be sure to clearly establish start and finish times with as much consistency as possible. Have coloring tools on hand if people want to continue to doodle as you discuss the passage.

Your job isn't to teach, and you don't have to have a ready answer for every question that comes up. It's okay to say, "I don't know" or "Does anyone have thoughts on that question?" Still, it's good to come prepared. As you review the session before your meeting, give some thought to the people in your group—what in the passage is likely to trip them up or cause them confusion? Which questions might touch on tender spots for them? How can you be a good support for your group members as the group is meeting?

Most of all, enjoy this time with one another. You are not alone in the leadership of this group; the Holy Spirit will be moving within you and your group members. Allow yourself grace as you lead, and look for opportunities to step aside and witness the Spirit at work.

May the creativity and reflection that this guide fosters lead to good discussion and rich friendships for you and your group!

NOTES FOR SESSION ONE

The book of Ruth doesn't come out and state whether Elimelech and his family were right to leave Bethlehem (see question 4), and we're not told what life was like in Moab. Historically Moab was a place of temptation to the people of Israel (see Numbers 25). Still, the Bible frequently tells stories of God's people temporarily relocating due to extenuating circumstances; even Jesus and his family fled to Egypt for a time when Herod sought to kill him as a child. The point of Elimelech's move to Moab is not necessarily whether the move itself was wise; the point is to showcase how vulnerable Naomi—and, by extension, Ruth and Orpah—were outside the Promised Land.

Naomi returns to Judah, the Scriptures tell us (see question 6), because "she had heard that GOD had been pleased to visit his people and give them food" (Ruth 1:6-7). In some ways Naomi is operating under the same utilitarian logic as Elimelech; she goes where the food is. But this passage is, tellingly, the first mention of God in the book of Ruth.

Naomi's complaint against God (see Ruth 1:19-22 and questions 13–16) is complicated. In some ways it resembles the cynical rant of someone who has rejected God. In context, however, Naomi has just returned to God's Promised Land because "she had heard that GOD had been pleased to visit his people" (see verses 6-7, 18-19).

So in some ways Naomi's complaint resembles a biblical lament: a complaint directed toward God in faith that he will respond. Consider sharing with the group other biblical complaints against God, from Moses to Job to the psalmist to the prophets, even Jacob wrestling an angel of the Lord until he received a blessing, or Jesus sweating blood at Gethsemane as he asked God to deliver him from crucifixion. This is not to preempt discussion about the appropriateness of Naomi's comments—some group members may feel strongly that she is dangerously disrespectful of God here—but lament is always uncomfortable to those who are not suffering. In any case, Naomi's complaint against God here will be answered lavishly in the chapters to come.

Some group members may not know what to do with feelings of anger toward God. Reassure the group that God is not surprised when we have negative feelings toward him, nor is he threatened by our negative feelings. As the arguments of Scripture show, God wants honesty between him and us; he will deal with the negative feelings with grace and truth. Worse than negative feelings toward God is avoidance or inauthenticity in relation to him.

NOTES FOR SESSION TWO

Gleaning (see question 6) was a provision in the law of Moses for poor people; landowners were to leave any crops that fell to the ground or otherwise went unharvested, so that the poor would be able to harvest food for themselves. The work of gleaning was hard and humbling, and yet it protected the dignity of poor people. Ruth worked very hard at gleaning, and while she had nothing and was a "Moabite foreigner" (Ruth 2:2), her esteem grew in the eyes of the people of Bethlehem (which means, in Hebrew, "house of bread").

Some of the virtues "coded into the book of Ruth" (question 12) might include hard work, generosity, charitableness, honesty, kindness, respectfulness, and loyalty.

NOTES FOR SESSION THREE

Naomi has a plan (question 4) that is based on the intricate social responsibilities woven into ancient Jewish culture. Family members had a fundamental responsibility toward one another's ability to flourish (see, for example, Deuteronomy 25:5-6). As we'll see in Ruth 4, these responsibilities were profound, to the point where a male relative of a man who died was required to be a "covenant redeemer"—to marry the dead man's widow and give her children in the dead man's name. (The marriage came with whatever assets the widow retained from her first marriage.) As we'll also see, Israelites were not averse to looking for loopholes, which meant that Naomi's plan—for Ruth to make herself available to Boaz as his wife—was not perfect. Even given this legal remedy, women were extremely vulnerable in ancient society. For an extreme example of this familial responsibility and attempts to avoid it, see Genesis 38. Theologically speaking, Jesus functions as our covenant redeemer, taking us as his bride and so saving us from ruin. He does so at great personal cost, but he does so willingly—no looking for loopholes for Jesus!

Some participants will read the statement in question 7 ("the harder you work, the luckier you get") as an endorsement of a kind of "bootstraps" mentality—that we are ultimately responsible for our circumstances. Of course that's not true; the Bible and our everyday life provide ample examples of people who have worked hard and lived well yet still struggle in any number of ways. Some participants, in fact, may bristle at question 7; they may see the premise of the question as an implicit judgment on them for whatever struggle they're facing. But by this point in the book of Ruth, she is clearly recognized as a person of character—hardworking, loyal to her mother-in-law, not entitled—and these virtues are clearly a factor in Boaz's esteem for her, which gives this unorthodox marriage proposal a good chance of success. In any case, the book of Ruth is not so much prescriptive as descriptive: It's telling a story within the epic narrative of God's work in the world, and Ruth's small acts of courage and virtue are critical elements in the story that's unfolding.

Question 12 draws our attention to the fact that this is a God-story, although God's role in the book of Ruth is somewhat hidden. Remind the group of Ruth's pledge to Naomi at the beginning of the story: "Your people are my people, your God is my god" (Ruth 1:16). This is Ruth the Moabite, whose people once led God's people astray into chaos (see Numbers 25); and yet now God's people have led this Moabite woman into hope and a future. It's because Ruth has been joined to the people of God that the law of Moses is providing for her needs. As we'll see in Ruth 4, God has done more than that: He's given Ruth a place in the story of King David, which gives her a place in the story of Jesus.

NOTES FOR SESSION FOUR

Remind the group of the basis and logistics of the "covenant redeemer" arrangement (see above; see also questions 4–7). Because this provision for widows is written into the Law, this negotiation of who will fulfill the obligation is appropriately done in public. But more than that, Israelite culture (and really, most of ancient culture and particularly Middle Eastern culture) was far more communally minded than our culture is today. The interests of the individual here are caught up in the interests of the community, as we have seen with the community's reception of Naomi in Ruth 1 and in their blessing of Boaz and Ruth here (Ruth 4:11-12).

The book of Ruth is both a small story and a big story (see question 12). It is small in that it takes place in the "little town of Bethlehem," with only a handful of characters, and with plot twists that, while significant in their context, are not earth-shattering. As a small story, the book of Ruth features three heroes (see question 8)— Naomi, who overcame her struggles and experienced restoration with God; Boaz, who was confronted with need and made sacrifices to meet the need; and Ruth, who came from obscurity and, with resilience and determination, provided a home and a future for herself and her family. But as a big story, we see God acting in mysterious ways to restore a prodigal woman (Naomi) to his people, to extend his grace and provision to a woman whose people were enemies to God's people (Ruth), and, through the marriage of Ruth and Boaz, to set up the lineage of Israel's greatest king (David)—who himself would be ancestor to Jesus, the Savior of the world. So God is undeniably a hero of this story as well (see question 9).

The prayer at the end of session four is repeated from session one. This prayer, now in retrospect, highlights the key themes of the book of Ruth: character and virtue, the importance of each person's story, the responsibility we have to one another, and the providence of God behind even the hard times we face.

DISCOVER THE DELIGHT OF BEING

Drawn in

From her simple faithfulness as a young woman to her soul-piercing anguish at the foot of the cross, journey with Mary through the sorrows and the joys of saying yes to God.

Ruth's resilience and resourcefulness offer you a creative vision for navigating life's inevitable struggles, trusting God, and holding fast to his irrevocable hope.

Esther's courage and conviction will help you discover how to find your voice and grow your faith during times of trouble.

Become the Woman
God Created You to Be

78-1-60006-663-4   978-1-57683-831-0   978-1-63146-564-2   978-1-61521-023-7   978-1-61521-021-3

Society beckons us to succeed—to achieve excellence in our appearance, our earning power, our family life. God Himself also beckons us to be women of excellence. But what exactly is He asking? If you're hungry for God's perspective on success, dig into God's Word with bestselling Bible teacher Cynthia Heald and experience the joy of becoming the woman God created you to be.

ADDITIONAL TITLES (NOT PICTURED):

Becoming a Woman of Grace
978-1-61521-022-0

Becoming a Woman of Strength
978-1-61521-620-8

Becoming a Woman of Freedom
978-1-57683-829-7

Becoming a Woman of Prayer
978-1-57683-830-3

Becoming a Woman Whose God Is Enough
978-1-61291-634-7